FLAMING OLYMPICS QUIZ BOOK

MICHAEL COLEMAN

www.michael-coleman.com

Illustrated by
Mike Phillips

■ SCHOLASTIC

Scholastic Children's Books,
Commonwealth House, 1-19 New Oxford Street
London WC1A 1NU, UK

A division of Scholastic Ltd
London ~ New York ~ Toronto ~ Sydney ~ Auckland
Mexico City ~ New Delhi ~ Hong Kong

First published in the UK by Scholastic Ltd, 2004

Text copyright © Michael Coleman, 2004
Illustrations copyright © Mike Phillips, 2004

ISBN 0 439 97749 5

All rights reserved
Printed and bound in Finland by WS Bookwell

2 4 6 8 10 9 7 5 3 1

CONTENTS

INTRODUCTION

With hundreds of different sports, thousands of competitors and millions of spectators, the Olympic Games is definitely the biggest sporting event on the planet.

The Olympic Games are so special they've even got their own Latin motto – *Citius, Altius, Fortius* – meaning: *Faster, Higher, Stronger.*

Why do the Olympics have this motto? Is it because you have to be good at computer games to take part?

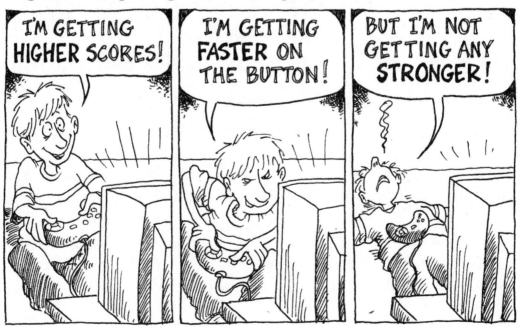

Is it because you have to be able to laze around all day?

Is it because you have to be a champion food-taster?

No, the motto was chosen because it describes what the Olympics Games are all about: sportsmen and sportswomen trying to do their best, whether they win or not. This is known as "The Olympic Ideal". It's the way it was when the Olympics first began – 3,000 years ago! Yes, what we now call the "ancient" Olympics took place in Greece in 776 BC. They lasted until AD 394 when they were scrapped. Why? Because competitors had forgotten all about the Olympic Ideal and were more concerned with dealing out bribes to help them win.

The Games stayed scrapped until a French aristocrat, Pierre de Coubertin, thought it was worth trying again. So began the "modern" Olympics, which were held for the first time – again in Greece – in 1896. They've now lasted for over 100 years. Will they survive for a thousand? That's just about the only question in this book you won't find an answer to!

What you *will* find are...
- awesome athletics questions
- boggling boxing questions
- sensational cycling questions.

In fact, there are questions (and answers) on just about every event that takes place in the Summer and Winter Olympics.

Will you be able to race through this book? Will you get a high score? Will your teachers be strong enough not to cry when they get the wrong answers – and you get the right ones?

There's only one way to find out. Let the Olympic Quiz Games begin!

OPENING CEREMONY

The first event at every Olympic Games isn't a sporting event at all. It's the opening ceremony – the spectacular event that officially gets the Games started. People scramble for tickets to be in the stadium to see it (even though, for the 2004 Games, each ticket cost up to £800!) and millions throughout the world tune in to watch it on TV – which is odd. Why? Because the same things happen every time! Yes, the opening ceremony has become a tradition…

For the very first time

Here are ten Olympic traditions, each dating from a different Olympic Games. Each of the games held between 1896 and 1936 is represented except for 1916 (when the Olympics weren't held because of World War One). Sort the traditions into date order, with the oldest first.

1896, 1900, 1904, 1908, 1912, 1920, 1924, 1928, 1932, 1936

1. Gold, silver and bronze medals for the first, second and third competitors in an event.
2. The Olympic flame, which burns throughout the Games.
3. The procession of competitors at the opening ceremony.
4. The Olympic flag with its white background and five interlocking rings coloured blue, black, red, yellow and green.
5. The torch relay, in which the Olympic flame is carried from Greece to the host country.
6. Teams representing different countries.
7. Women competitors.
8. The medal presentation podium, with its first, second and third positions.
9. The first separate Winter Olympics.
10. The first Olympics Games to take place outside Europe.

Answers:

1896 – 3. the procession of competitors. For the first-ever Games, this was more of a stroll than a procession. Nowadays, there's a strict order. Greece is always first, in recognition of being the country which began it all; then come the other teams, in alphabetical order. The host country comes last.

1900 – 7. women competitors. All 19 of them!

1904 – 10. outside Europe, as in St Louis, USA. The Games weren't a great success because they were combined with a world fair and spread out over a period of five months!

1908 – 1. gold, silver and bronze medals. In earlier games, only winners and runners-up received prizes. The winner got a silver medal, a certificate and an olive branch. The runner-up got a copper medal and a sprig of laurel.

1912 – 6. teams representing different countries. Before this competitors entered as individuals.

1920 – 4. the Olympic flag. The five colours were chosen because, in 1920, at least one of them appeared in the flag of each country taking part.

1924 – 9. the first Winter Olympics. That is, the Winter Olympics became a totally separate event from what was now known as the Summer Olympics. This isn't to say that "winter" sports hadn't been seen before: figure-skating had been an Olympic event since 1908!

1928 – 2. the Olympic flame. Lit during the opening ceremony, the flame stays alight until the closing ceremony (unless the gas is cut off earlier!).

1932 – 8. the medal presentation podium. Until now, there'd usually been a simple one-level platform in front of the guest of honour. The athletes had gone to him (it always had been a him) to get their medals. Now, he was forced to shift himself and come to the athletes instead.

1936 – 5. the torch relay. It covered 3,000 km, with the torch being carried by 3,000 torch-bearers running 1 km each.

Did you know?

Memorabilia from the Olympics are often sold off when the event is over. Following the Sydney 2000 Games, for example, you could have bid for one of two medal presentation podiums in an Internet auction. Starting price – £500!

WHY COULDN'T YOU HAVE BID FOR THE TORCH?

Torch truth

Sort out the fact from the fiction with these statements about Olympic-torch relays.

11. Before 2004, the highest number of torch-bearers used in one Olympic games was 13,300 for the Sydney 2000 Olympics. **True or False?**

12. The whole idea for the torch relay came from a fun relay race at the ancient Olympics in which teams had to pass on a flaming torch instead of a baton. **True or False?**

13. In 1956, an Italian named Guido Caroli had the honour of carrying the Olympic flame into the Olympic arena – but instead of running in, he arrived on skates. **True or False?**

14. Caroli also became the first torch-bearer to do a spin before handing over the flame. **True or False?**

15. In 2000, the torch was plunged into water on its way round Australia – but the flame didn't go out! **True or False?**

16. In 1948, during its journey from Greece to London, the Olympic torch took a detour to visit Pierre de Coubertin's house. **True or False?**

17. The first Australian torch-bearer to carry the 2000 Olympic flame was an athlete named Nova Peris Kneebone. **True or False?**

Answers:

11. False. The highest number to date is the 101,473 torch-bearers used to carry the Olympic flame from Greece to Tokyo in 1964.

12. True. The race was called the *lampadedromia* (meaning – guess what? – torch race!). The first team home with the torch still alight won the race. Their prize? The honour of lighting the sacred Olympic flame.

13. True. Gliding Guido was arriving for the flame-lighting ceremony at the ice rink used for the Winter Olympics at Cortina d'Ampezzo in Italy.

14. False. Gormless Guido famously fell over. It wasn't all his fault, though. A cable had been left trailing across the rink and he didn't see it. Great Guido turned disaster into triumph, though. Still clutching the torch, he recovered his footing and carried on.

15. True. The flame's route through Australia took in the famous Great Barrier Reef Marine Park off the north Queensland coast. There it travelled under water, staying alight because it was fitted with a specially invented underwater flare.

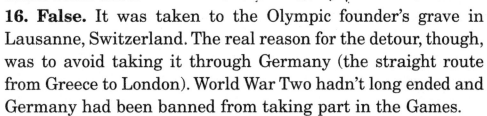

16. False. It was taken to the Olympic founder's grave in Lausanne, Switzerland. The real reason for the detour, though, was to avoid taking it through Germany (the straight route from Greece to London). World War Two hadn't long ended and Germany had been banned from taking part in the Games.

17. True. Nova Kneebone, an Aboriginal athlete, received the honour because the 100-day journey round Australia began in the Aboriginal lands at Uluru-Kata Tjuta National Park.

Now, nearly – and never!

Olympic sports and events are a bit like pop songs. Some are classics that seem like they've always been around and always will be. Others are popular for a while, then fade away – and then there are those that get nowhere near the charts because even the cat can't stand the noise!

In each of the following groups of three events...
- one is in the Olympics **NOW**
- one **NEARLY** made it, but was thrown out after a while
- and the third has **NEVER** been an Olympic event.

Sort out which is which.

18. a) Rope-climbing.
b) Rhythmic gymnastics.
c) Lasso-spinning.

19. a) Cricket.
b) Snooker.
c) Baseball.

20. a) White-water canoeing.
b) Waterskiing.
c) Motorboat racing.

21. a) Women's croquet.
b) Women's football.
c) Women's wrestling.

22. a) Skeet shooting.
b) Tin-can shooting.
c) Live-pigeon shooting.

23. a) Arm-wrestling.
b) Super-heavyweight weightlifting.
c) Tug-of-war.

24. a) Golf.
b) Ten-pin bowling.
c) Beach volleyball.

25. a) Water ballet.
b) Bomb-diving.
c) Underwater swimming.

Answers:
18. NOW: b) Rhythmic gymnastics – a women's-only event featuring gymnasts jumping through hoops and doing somersaults while they twirl ribbons. **NEARLY: a)** Rope-climbing was an on-and-off event in Olympic gymnastics until 1932. **NEVER: c)** Lasso-spinning.
19. NOW: c) Baseball. **NEARLY: a)** Cricket, which was bowled out after its only appearance in 1900. **NEVER: b)** Snooker.
20. NOW: a) White-water canoeing (also known as the canoe slalom). **NEARLY: c)** Motorboat racing, which made its only appearance in 1908 before being sunk. **NEVER: b)** Waterskiing.
21. NOW: b) Women's football. **NEARLY: a)** Women's croquet. The game was played at the 1900 Olympics only. It was one of the first events that women were allowed to compete in. The winner was Margaret Abbott of the USA, who was said to have been helped because "all the French girls misunderstood the nature of the game and turned up to play in tight skirts and high heels". **NEVER: c)** Women's wrestling.

CROQUET NOT CROCHET!

22. NOW: a) Skeet shooting. A "skeet" isn't a thing, it's a type of competition. The shooter has to hit "clay pigeons", which are catapulted from side to side and at different heights. **NEARLY: c)** Live-pigeon shooting. Sorry, this really was an event in 1900. Even worse, the Belgian winner, Leon de Lunden, hit 21 of them. **NEVER: b)** Tin-can shooting.

23. NOW: b) Super-heavyweight weightlifting. The "super-heavyweight" refers to the weight of the competitor, not how much they lift! Super-heavies weigh in at over 105 kg! **NEARLY: c)** Tug-of-war. This was an athletics event until 1920. It was then tugged out of the Games and hasn't returned. **NEVER: a)** Arm-wrestling.

24. NOW: c) Beach volleyball. **NEARLY: a)** Golf, which made its (hole-in-)one and only appearance in the 1900 Olympics. **NEVER: b)** Ten-pin bowling.

25. NOW: a) Water ballet (which is what synchronized swimming was called when it was invented in Canada in the 1920s). **NEARLY: c)** Underwater swimming. This appeared – don't hold your breath – just once, in 1900. The winner was Charles de Vendeville, from France, who swam an incredible 157 metres before coming up for air! **NEVER: b)** Bomb-diving.

Did you know?
Whatever your sport, if you weren't judged fit enough one month before the ancient Olympics were due to start then you weren't allowed to compete.

PROVE YOU'RE FIT. TOUCH YOUR TOES.

WHAT TOES?

WATER PERFORMANCE!

Strangely, water sports didn't feature in the ancient Olympics – strange, because swimming was an activity well known to many of the world's ancient civilizations. Julius Caesar, for instance, was famous for his swimming prowess.

The famous epic Greek poem, *The Odyssey*, mentions swimming as well. So why there's no record of any ancient Olympians' water-sport victories being splashed all over the ancient front pages is something of an unfathomable mystery.

The modern Olympics didn't hesitate to take the plunge, though, and watery events have been included ever since the Games were refloated in 1896. And now, as the real Games starts with events that are called "Aquatics", we're opening with a section about these sports too. Here's a quick question to get you started:

26. Which of these Olympic sports *isn't* included in the "Aquatics" category?
a) Diving.
b) Swimming.
c) Sailing.
d) Synchronized swimming.
e) Water polo.

Aquatics antics

Even though they're in the water, aquatics competitors don't always find life plain sailing! Match these performers with the problems they faced...

27. In 1936, Eleanor Holm (USA) was the reigning 100 m backstroke champion – but she wasn't allowed to compete after being found guilty of this. (clue: in the drink)

a) Using an asthma inhaler.

28. Ethelda Bleibtrey (USA) won three gold medals in world-record times at the 1920 Olympics – just one year after being arrested for this. (clue: she wasn't skinny, not really)

b) Finishing in a slower time.

29. Greg Louganis of the USA won gold for springboard diving in 1988 – even after doing this. (clue: tough nut)

c) Getting drunk on a boat.

30. Dawn Fraser (Australia) won the women's 100 m freestyle in 1956, 1960 and 1964 – after spending her childhood in this way. (clue: take a deep breath)

d) Swimming in the nude.

31. Brazil's water polo team was disqualified in 1932 for doing this. (clue: too many peeps!)

e) Suffering from asthma.

32. Greta Andersen (Denmark) had won the 1948 100 m freestyle but in the 400 m she found herself doing this. (clue: floating feeling)

f) Winning more golds in one Games than her whole country ever had before.

33. In 1972 Rick DeMont (USA) won, then lost, the 400 m freestyle gold after doing this. (clue: take another deep breath)

g) Hitting his head on a board.

34. A tight finish between John Devitt (Australia) and Lance Larson (USA) in the 1960 men's 100 m freestyle ended with Devitt winning gold – in spite of this. (clue: stop the clock!)

h) Fainting during the race.

35. At the 1996 Olympics, Ireland's Michelle Smith set a record by doing this. (clue: gold rush)

i) Insulting the referee.

Answers:

27. c) – not once, but often, during the American team's Atlantic voyage to the 1936 Games in Berlin, Germany. In her own defence, entertaining Eleanor – who was a rich lady – argued: "The team regulations tell us to use the same training methods on the voyage as we do at home. Well, at home I simply always have a glass or two of champagne after training!"

28. d) – but not during the Olympics! It had happened at a public beach … when bold Bleibtrey had done nothing ruder than remove her stockings!

29. g) – the board in question being the diving board he'd just jumped from. Leaping high into the air and launching into a backwards somersault, the diver hit the board with the back of his head on his way down. It looked like he was destined to be Louganis the loser, but no. He completed the rest of his dives to become Greg the Golden.

30. e) – one of the reasons fantastic Fraser took up swimming was that she found the swimming pool atmosphere helped her breathe easier.

31. i) – they'd just lost 3-7 to Germany, the eventual silver-medallists. *(No reason for calling the referee a big drip!)*

32. h) – groggy Greta had to be helped from the pool. When the results were announced she'd sunk to the bottom!

33. a) – DeMont won the race but was stripped of the gold medal when it was discovered he had unknowingly used an asthma inhaler containing a banned drug. Raging Rick showed them what he could do the following year, winning the 400 m World Championship in the first-ever under-4-minute swim. (To this day, DeMont is still trying to clear his name and get his confiscated medal back from the International Olympic Committee.)

34. b) – in 1960, the judges' decision was what mattered, and they announced that Devitt had just beaten Larson … only to learn that the electronic timing devices had made Larson 0.1

seconds faster! From then on, the judges' opinion was jettisoned and electronic times were used to decide the winners.

35. f) – mercurial Michelle came through from nowhere to outdo every Irish team in Olympic history and win three golds and a bronze. Her successes were controversial though, with many accusing her of taking drugs. Sweet Smith denied it. Two years later, though, she was banned – for trying to fiddle a drugs test. Hmm.

Plunging pairs

Here's a quiz that gives you two tests for the price of one – well, one sentence, anyway. Buried in each of the following invented sentences are two phrases related in some way to aquatic events. You may be looking for the names of competitors, of events – anything. The introduction to each sentence tells you exactly what sort of watery words you're after. Can you fish them out?

36. A pair of two-word swimming events from years gone by: "I don't fancy diving," said Walter Duck-Down. "All those rocks make it a dangerous dip; more of an obstacle course than a safe swim."

37. These are seen in Olympic swimming pools but made their first appearances 60 years apart: "During an amazing punch-up between high-board divers, relay swimmers and synchronized swimmers, judges had to leap into the water and act as lane dividers!"

38. The nicknames for two swimmers who took part in the Sydney 2000 Games: "Prize exhibits in the sea-life zoo are Sally the Shark, Eric the Eel, Paula the Porpoise, Oliver the Octopus and Willy the Whale."

39. Two locations used for Olympic swimming events: "The old White City Athletics Stadium was a lot closer to the River Thames than it was to either the Seine or the Amazon."

40. Two famous medal-winning swimmers: "Excited celebrity-spotters outside the VIP tent were rewarded by the appearances of the Duke of Hawaii, the Queen of Sheba, the Little Princess and the Lord of the Jungle."

Answers:

36. Fancy diving was the name given in 1908 to diving that involved somersaults and that sort of thing. (It's now just "diving", of course). **Obstacle course** was an event that made its one appearance in 1900. It was a 200 m race in which the swimmers had to get over and under a row of upturned boats!

37. Synchronized swimmers made their first appearance at the Olympics in 1984. **Lane dividers**, running the length of the pool to keep swimmers apart, were first introduced 60 years previously, in 1924.

38. Eric the Eel was the name given to Eric Moussambani of Equatorial Guinea after he swam one of the slowest 100 m freestyles in Olympic history – and still won his heat! The other two swimmers in his heat had been disqualified and Eric had swum alone. **Paula the Porpoise** was the only other member of Equatorial Guinea's swimming team – and she swam even slower! By the time she'd finished her 50 m women's freestyle heat, the winner could have done another length. Paula had spent just six weeks training, in a river near her village.

39. White City Athletics Stadium – for the 1908 Games a 100 m pool was constructed alongside the athletics track (which itself was inside the cycling track!). **The Seine** was the "pool" used for the swimming events in 1900.

40. Duke of Hawaii – the 100 m freestyle in 1912 was won by Duke Paoa Kahanamoku, a descendant of the Hawaiian king. He was representing the USA because Hawaii had become one of the US states in 1898. **Lord of the Jungle** – the winner of five swimming gold medals in 1924 and 1928, Johnny Weissmuller (USA) went on to star in more than a dozen films as Tarzan, Lord of the Jungle!

Did you know?
If you're a girl with a twin sister, then the best Olympic sport for you to take up is definitely synchronized swimming. In the pairs event at the 2000 Games four out of the 24 couples taking part were twins.

MINE SHOULD BE TEN MINUTES OLDER THAN HERS

Onboard or overboard

Try these teasers on Olympic events that involve "boats" of different types – but don't scupper your chances of a good score by ignoring the clues hidden in the questions!

41. Which bubbly new event was taken on board in the Olympics of 1972?

a) White-water canoeing.

b) Windsurfing.

42. Rowers in the 1904 Games had to cover a distance of 1.5 miles – but what strange feature of the course really had them doubled up in pain while they were on board?

a) It was S-shaped.

b) It was U-shaped.

43. A Russian rower, Vyacheslav Ivanov, dropped something overboard at the 1956 Games – and it wasn't an "oarsome" thing to do. What did he drop?

a) A medal.

b) An oar.

44. In 1900, a Dutch crew decided to replace something they'd had on board during a race – because they thought it was weighing them down. Was it:

a) A lifebuoy.

b) A live body.

45. Crown Prince Constantine of Greece, a yachting competitor at the 1960 Olympics, felt rather down after meeting his mother, Queen Frederika. Why?
a) He'd just won his race.
b) He'd just lost his race.

46. The weather caused Canadian sailor Lawrence Mimieux to stop racing when he was in with a good chance of a medal at the 1988 Olympics – even though the race took place in September, not on a May day. What had been the problem?
a) Strong winds.
b) No wind at all.

47. After their yacht broke down for the third time at the 1976 Olympics in Montreal, British yachtsmen Alan Warren and David Hunt had a spark of an idea about what to do about their craft. What?
a) Turn it into a powerboat.
b) Set fire to it.

48. After gunning his way to a fourth gold medal in 1996, exhausted British rower Steve (now Sir Steve) Redgrave announced live on TV: "Anybody who sees me go near a boat after this has permission to .... me!" What's the missing word?
a) Kiss.
b) Shoot.
c) Sink.
d) Board.

Answers:

41. a) White-water canoeing, in which competitors have to steer a canoe between posts while shooting the rapids! Windsurfing didn't make its first appearance until 1988 as a demonstration event.

42. b) The rowers had to make a turn so that they finished where they started. They couldn't have known whether they were coming or going!

43. a) The gold medal he'd just won for the single sculls event! Ivanov had thrown it up in excitement but failed to catch it before it sank to the bottom of Lake Wendouree in Australia. Water idiot!

44. b) It was the body of their cox (the person who steers the boat), who they'd decided was slowing them down because he was too heavy. Instead they recruited a young boy (not buoy!) from the watching crowd and with him on board they won the coxed pairs final by just 0.2 seconds!

45. a) The prince was a member of the Greek team that took the gold in the Dragon class yachting. Mum handed over his medal – then helped out with the traditional ducking for the winners.

Did you know?

The first-ever royal gold medallist was King Olav of Norway, who was a member of the Norwegian crew that triumphed in the 6 m yacht class in 1928.

46. a) The bad weather had caused havoc and two Singaporean sailors, in another race entirely, had been badly injured. Ignoring the fact that he was in second position in his own race, Mimieux went to their aid and stayed with them until they were rescued. It was later agreed that if anybody deserved a medal he did, and Lawrence the lifesaver was given a special award.

47. b) It gave a whole new meaning to the idea of an "Olympic flame"!

48. b) Fortunately for Redgrave, nobody took him seriously – which meant that he was able to win a record fifth gold medal in the Sydney 2000 Games.

MARATHON MYSTERIES

Perhaps the most famous event at the Olympics is the marathon. It's so well known that the word has found its way into dictionaries. Check the one in your classroom. It probably says something like:

Marathon Any lengthy and difficult task (noun); requiring or displaying great powers of endurance (adjective).

You may think it's a good word to describe how you feel about doing your homework, but does that really compare to an Olympic marathon? It's a road race (even though it starts and finishes on the athletics track) run over the strange distance of 26 miles and 385 yards (42.2 km).

49. Who decided that the marathon should be this mysterious length?
a) An Italian count.
b) An English princess.
c) A French aristocrat.

Answer:
49. b) Princess Mary, when the Olympics were held in London in 1908, asked if the marathon could finish beneath the royal box at the White City stadium. This added another 385 yards to the planned 26-mile race … and it's stayed that way ever since.

ER...ACTUALLY, THE FINISH IS OVER THERE

Finish or fail

That extra little bit of distance has proved to be a real problem for some runners. Sort out the tottering truth in this collection. Did the runners finish – or fail?

50. In that same year, 1908, Italian Dorando Pietri was presented with a cup instead of a medal. **Finish or Fail?**

51. It's 1948, again in London, and Etienne Gailly of Belgium was in the lead as he entered Wembley Stadium with only 385 yards to go. **Finish or Fail?**

52. In the 1912 marathon in Stockholm, the Japanese runner Shizo Kanakuri collapsed with heat exhaustion. He'd promised himself that he'd finish the race, though. **Finish or Fail?**

53. Another Japanese marathon runner, Kokichi Tsuburaya, was determined to win the race for his country when the Games were held in Tokyo in 1964. **Finish or Fail?**

54. In 1904, American Thomas Hicks was nearing the finish when somebody gave him some poison to drink. **Finish or Fail?**

55. During the first-ever modern marathon in 1896, Edwin Flack of Australia was kept supplied with drinks by his own bicycle-riding butler! **Finish or Fail?**

56. In 1972, the first runner into the stadium was Norbert Sudhous. Behind him, though, other runners were closing fast. Did Sudhous **Finish or Fail?**

57. Fred Lorz of the USA was first man out of the stadium at the start of the 1904 marathon – and first in again at the end of the race. Did he **Finish or Fail?**

Answers:

50. Fail. Pietri collapsed five times on the track (almost in front of the royal box!). He only managed to cross the finishing line with the help of the race starter, which was enough to get him disqualified. Queen Alexandra felt so sorry for Pietri (or embarrassed about her daughter's suggestion) that she awarded him his own cup as a consolation prize.

51. Finish – but only in third place. After 26 miles, he was overtaken by two other runners in the final 385 yards.

52. Finish (after Fail). Kanakuri dropped out of the 1912 race, but returned to the Olympic stadium in 1967 to run the final lap he'd missed all those years before. So his time for the race was 54 years, 8 months, 2 days, 32 minutes and 20.3 seconds!

53. Finish – but only in third place. Tsuburaya considered this a Fail and that he'd let his country down. He vowed to make up for it at the 1968 Olympics. When he got injured and realized he wouldn't be able to take part, he committed suicide. He left the saddest of messages: "Cannot run any more." There's now a charity in his name, the Tsuburaya Memorial Fund, which was set up to help runners anywhere in the world.

54. Finish – first! The poison was strychnine, which is only deadly if you take a lot of it. A little bit is helpful – which is why Hicks's coach gave it to him.

55. Fail. He couldn't even raise the energy to get on the butler's bike, he felt so tyred!

56. Fail – to the spectators' delight. Sudhous was a hoaxer who'd stripped down to his underwear just before the real runners arrived at the stadium, then ran round the track until the pursuing and red-faced security guards caught up with him.

57. Finish and Fail – because Lorz hadn't run the bit in the middle. After suffering from cramp, he'd stopped running, got a lift to the stadium, then started running again! Lorz didn't run much after that, though. He was banned for life.

The last gasp game

Running marathons leaves you pretty short of breath, so it's hard to say much. Even so, here are some things marathon runners have managed to say – except that some words have come out as GASP. Replace the GASPs by words from this list to find out what the runners really said.

boring, drink, faster, rejoice, wait, walk

58. The marathon race itself commemorates a run supposedly made by a Greek messenger called Pheidippides in 490 BC to tell everybody that their army had conquered the Persians with the words: "GASP! We conquer!"

59. The 1952 marathon was won by Emil Zatopek of Czechoslovakia. He told a reporter afterwards: "The marathon really is a very GASP race."

60. In the same race, Zatopek turned to British runner Jim Peters, one of the favourites, and asked: "Don't you think we ought to go GASP?"

61. South Africans Christian Gitsham and Kenneth McArthur were leading the 1912 marathon when Gitsham said: "I must stop for a GASP."

62. Sportingly, McArthur replied: "I'll GASP for you."

63. Joan Benoit (USA) became the first-ever winner of the women's marathon, taking the 1984 Los Angeles gold. Afterwards, she talked about how it all began: "When I first started running I was so embarrassed I'd GASP when cars passed me."

Answers:

58. "**REJOICE! We conquer!**" They were also Pheidippides' last words, because after gasping them he collapsed and died. Why? Because he'd run from the Plain of Marathon to Athens, a total distance of 280 km!

59. "**The marathon really is a very BORING race.**" That could explain why Zatopek broke the then world record by six minutes – he was fed up and wanted to go home!

60. "**Don't you think we ought to go FASTER?**" said Zatopek, explaining tongue-in-cheek (a clever trick while you're running!) that this was his first marathon.

61. "**I must stop for a DRINK,**" said Gitsham as they approached a refreshment point.

62. "**I'll WAIT for you,**" said McArthur – except that mean McArthur didn't. Instead, he quickly ran off again to win the race and leave gurgling Gitsham to take second place almost a minute behind.

63. "**When I first started running, I was so embarrassed I'd WALK when cars passed me,**" said bashful Benoit, adding, "I'd pretend I was looking at the flowers."

The tottering ten

The history of the marathon is littered with so many staggering tales it's not always easy to see which runner is going to stagger in the winner. See if you can do it. In this tottering ten there are five winners and five losers. But which are which?

64. At the marathon medal ceremony in 1936, he bowed his head in sorrow as the Japanese national anthem was played.

65. In 1904, he ran in his own shoes and a pair of trousers with the legs cut off.

66. At the medal ceremony in 1964, he beamed with surprised pride as the Japanese national anthem was played.

67. During the race in 1900, he was forced to ask a policeman which way to go.

68. Five weeks before the 1964 marathon, he'd had a pain in the stomach.

69. He had a pain in the stomach during the 1980 race.

70. She was trapped in a department store while, outside, the 1984 marathon was starting.

THIS ONE'S ALIVE!

71. During the 1904 race, he had to cope with having two pursuers on his tail.

72. At the 1960 Games in Rome, he stopped well away from the athletics stadium and couldn't carry on.

73. In 1908, he celebrated with the glass of champagne he was offered.

Answers:

64. WINNER. Sohn Kee-Chung had been forced to run for Japan because his country (Korea) had been invaded by the Japanese. All was put right for him in 1988, though, when the Olympics were held in a now-independent South Korea. Sohn, then aged 76, carried the flame into the stadium, proudly wearing his Korean running vest.

65. LOSER – but one of the most gallant ever. Feliz Carvajal had lost all his belongings on the way to America from Cuba and had to run in the clothes he'd left in. He came fourth!

66. WINNER. Abebe Bikila came from Ethiopia but the band hadn't known the Ethiopian anthem so they'd played the Japanese one instead.

67. LOSER. Ernst Fast of Sweden came third – the policeman sent him the wrong way!

68. WINNER. Abebe Bikila in 1964 again. Five weeks before the race he'd needed to have his appendix taken out.

69. LOSER. This was the Finnish runner, Lasse Viren, who then had to dive behind some bushes for a poo. It didn't help, though, and the rest of Viren dropped out of the race soon after.

70. WINNER. Joan Benoit, the 1984 women's champion, used to have this nightmare.

71. LOSER. In the 1904 marathon in St Louis, Len Tau, one of the first two Africans to compete at the Olympics, was chased a mile off course by two dogs. He still managed to finish ninth – so you have to admit that Len was a really dogged competitor!

STRANGE WAY OF TAKING YOUR DOGS FOR A WALK!

72. WINNER. Abebe Bikila (him again!) came to a halt well away from the stadium because – unusually – the 1960 race started on Rome's Capitoline Hill and ended at the Arch of Constantine, both outside the stadium.

73. LOSER. Unfortunately, it was during the race that Charles Hefferon of South Africa was leading. It made him feel all woozy and he ended up finishing second!

ON TRACK

Out of all the many sporting events, running track athletics is probably the one most associated with the Olympic Games. This should be no surprise. In the ancient Games a foot race was the first-ever event to take place.

So, as it all started on the track, having a quiz about starts and tracks is the obvious way to begin this section!

Start here

74. At the ancient Olympics, the shortest-distance foot race was called the "stade". About how far did the athletes have to run?

a) 100 m.
b) 200 m.
c) 400 m.

75. How far was one lap of the track at the 1896 Olympics in Athens?

a) 333.33 m.
b) 444.44 m.
c) 555.55 m.

76. How many bends did the 200 m runners have to negotiate in 1904?

a) None.
b) One.
c) Two.

77. When Britain's Eric Liddell won the 400 m in 1924, his world-record time wasn't officially recognized because of the track. What was wrong with it?

a) Wrong shape.
b) Wrong surface.
c) Wrong length.

78. The runners' lanes for the 100 m in London in 1908 were made from – what?
a) Paint.
b) String.
c) Canes.

79. The track caused a big punch-up in 1908 during a 400 m race. What didn't it have?

STARTING BLOCKS | RUNNERS' LANES | A FINISHING LINE

80. What was the starter's first job at the ancient Olympics?
a) To shout.
b) To point.
c) To scratch.

81. At the start of one of the 100 m heats at the 1896 Games, Danish sprinter Eugen Schmidt was helped by leaning on two – what?
a) Sticks.
b) Officials.
c) Blocks.

82. False starts have always been frowned on. What happened to a runner who committed one at the ancient Games?
a) He was disqualified.
b) He was stripped naked.
c) He was flogged.

83. What punishment was dished out to runners who committed a false start at the 1904 Olympics?
a) They were disqualified.
b) They were sent away.
c) They were forgiven.

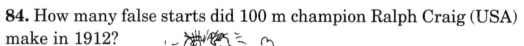

84. How many false starts did 100 m champion Ralph Craig (USA) make in 1912?
a) One.
b) Two.
c) Three.

Answers:
74. b) – 192.27 m to be precise. The stade was a straight race down the length of the arena (which is why it became known as the "stadium").
75. a) – it was also modelled on the track of the ancient Games stadium, being long and thin, with two very sharp turns at either end. The Olympics weren't held on a 400 m track until 1920.
76. a) – in 1904, the 200 m was held on a special straight section of track.
77. c) – by then, 400 m running tracks had become standard, but the track in Paris was 500 m in length. This meant that in covering 400 m, Liddell had only had to go round one bend instead of two. As running a bend usually takes longer, his record wasn't allowed.
78. b) and c) – lengths of string were stretched between canes stuck in the surface of the track.
79. b) – the made-up lanes weren't used for other races. So when, in the 400 m, Wyndham Halswelle was trying to overtake his rival, American John Carpenter, there was nothing to stop Carpenter from moving out to block his way – which he apparently did! A rerun was ordered, but Carpenter and the other two qualifiers (also Americans) refused to run,

giving Halswelle the only Olympic walkover in a running race! After that, all tracks were given lanes.

80. c) – the starter would scratch a line in the earth of the track for all the runners to stand behind. It's where we get our saying: to start from scratch!

81. a) – starting blocks hadn't been invented. Some sprinters stood up, some knelt down. Schmidt did a bit of both. He leaned on two sticks about 10 cm long, leaving them behind when he started running.

82. a) and c). He was **b)** already, because runners at the ancient Olympics performed in the nude.

Did you know?

Apart from the danger of being flogged for a false start, runners at the ancient Games had to cope with a harsh rule at the other end of the track. Unlike the modern Olympics, a dead heat didn't give both athletes equal first place. Instead, neither of them won. The race was declared not to have a winner.

83. b) They were sent away by about a metre for every false start they made – meaning they had to run further than everybody else. This was great for Archie Hahn (USA) in the 100 m final. His three opponents helped him win the race by all having false starts!

84. c) Nowadays it's two false starts and you're off – the track!

Go, girls!

These days, the women's track programme is as extensive as the men's. But it wasn't always the case. In 1896, there were no women's track events at all.

The founder of the modern Olympics, French aristocrat Pierre de Coubertin, had fixed ideas about the part ladies might play. He said: "Women have but one task, that of ..."

85. How did the baron complete his sentence?

a) ... making the sandwiches.
b) ... polishing the medals.
c) ... crowning the winner with garlands.

Answer:
85. c)

By the 1928 Olympics, de Coubertin had stopped being one of the organizers. That year women competed in athletics events for the first time: the 100 m, 800 m, 4 x 100 m relay, discus and high jump were all on the programme. That didn't stop him saying his piece, though...

86. After the women's 800 m, de Coubertin complained that the tired women provided – what?
a) A very unedifying spectacle for the spectators.
b) Convincing proof that their legs weren't made for running.
c) Extremely poor value for money.

What would Baron de Coubertin think if he were around today? Here's a test to help you form your own opinion. Decide how many of the women gold-medal winners at the hundredth anniversary Olympics in 1996 would have won medals in the men's events in 1924 – the last Olympics of which de Coubertin was in charge? Answer gold, silver, bronze – or none.

	EVENT	WINNER	TIME
87	100 m	GAIL DEVERS	10·94
88	200 m	MARIE-JOSE PEREC	22·12
89	400 m	MARIE-JOSE PEREC	48·25
90	800 m	SVETLANA MASTERKOVA	1:57·73
91	1500 m	SVETLANA MASTERKOVA	4:00·83
92	5,000 m	WANG JUNXIA	14:59·88
93	10,000 m	FERNANDA RIBEIRO	31:01·63
94	MARATHON	FATUMA ROBA	2:26:05
95	400 m HURDLES	DEON HEMMINGS	52·82
96	4 X 100 m RELAY	USA	41·95
97	4 X 400 m RELAY	USA	3:20·91

Judging from these results, there's not much doubt that, if he was around today, belligerent Baron de Coubertin would become red-faced, embarrassed de Coubertin!

Last seen wearing

If you're not going to win your race, one way of getting noticed is to wear something eye-catching. Here's a selection of items that have been seen on Olympic tracks – except that the owners have become mixed up. Use the clues to return each item to the rightful athlete.

98. Boyd Gittens, running in a USA 100 m hurdles trial, didn't foresee the freak accident that caused him to lose one of the <u>long fingernails</u> he was wearing.

99. Paavo Nurmi of Finland had time on his hands when he ran the 10,000 m in 1952 carrying <u>a woman</u>.

100. Michael Johnson (USA) stormed to first place in the 1996 200 m wearing his trademark <u>old golf cap</u>.

101. In 2000, Australian women's 400 m champion Cathy Freeman (Australia) turned back the clock by copying an ancient Olympic tradition and wearing <u>nothing</u>.

102. Gail Devers (USA) clawed her way to 100 m wins in 1992 and 1996 wearing ten <u>running vests</u>.

103. Abebe Bikila of Ethiopia showed a clean pair of heels to the other marathon runners in 1960 by wearing <u>white shorts</u> on his feet.

104. In 1972, Dave Wottle of the USA had to head straight for a studio to apologize on TV for receiving his 800 m gold medal while still wearing his <u>kangaroo hide</u>.

105. The Jamaican 4 x 100 m relay team runners were almost counted out of their final in 1952. They only had three <u>contact lenses</u> between them.

106. The same applied to the American 3,000 m steeplechase runners in 1908. They were very short-tempered after being told that they would not be allowed to race until they swapped their <u>gold running shoes</u> for dark ones.

107. Emil Zatopek of Czechoslovakia, who won the 10,000 m in 1948 and, in 1952, the 5,000 m, 10,000 m and the marathon, regularly trained by wearing <u>a stopwatch</u> on his back.

108. Australia's 1,500 m winner in 1960, Herb Elliott, bounded round the track in a pair of running shoes made from a <u>white sheet</u>.

109. Elliott's trainer, Percy Cerutty, was also kitted out. If Elliott was wide awake and running at the right speed, he'd agreed to wave <u>a suit with a helmet</u>.

Answers:

98. <u>contact lenses.</u> It was knocked out by a pigeon dropping! Boyd was given a rerun and qualified for the team.

99. <u>a stopwatch.</u> Nurmi did this in every race he ran, only throwing the watch infield when he started his final spurt for the finishing line.

100. <u>gold running shoes.</u> Johnson also broke the world record with an amazing 200 m time of 19.32 seconds.

101. <u>a suit with a helmet.</u> It wasn't quite as they did it at the ancient Games, though. There, the soldier's race had the competitors carrying a shield and wearing a helmet – but the suits they were wearing were their birthday suits!

102. <u>long fingernails.</u> They were about 5 cm long! But the gallant Gail had "claws" to be happy. Years before, she'd been so ill she was in danger of having one of her legs amputated.

103. <u>nothing.</u> Tough-toes Bikila ran all 26 miles and 385 yards barefooted.

104. <u>old golf cap.</u> Wottle was so used to wearing it to run in, he forgot to take it off for the medal ceremony.

105. <u>running vests.</u> Quick thinking led to a quick change between the first runner, Arthur Wint, and the fourth runner, George Rhoden – and a quick time. The Jamaicans broke the world record and won the gold!

106. <u>white shorts</u>. They were against the rules at that time because the judges thought they were harder to see.

107. <u>a woman</u>. Mrs Zatopek, to be precise – who was no lightweight herself. She won the women's javelin in the 1952 Olympics!

108. <u>kangaroo-hide</u>. Obviously the kangaroo didn't bound fast enough, though.

109. <u>white sheet</u>. Cerutty did it – and was promptly arrested for trespassing on the track. Elliott won the race in a world-record time, then had to spend hours pleading for his coach to be released from the police station!

Did you know?

The most obscure running accessory was probably that used by Forest Smithson in 1908. He showed his displeasure at the final of the 110 m hurdles being held on a Sunday by being pictured with a Bible in his left hand. Somebody was certainly on his side – Smithson won, in world-record time.

I THINK HE'S TAKING THIS PROTEST A BIT TOO FAR!

Against the odds

The Olympics are littered with tales of heroism. Here are just a few from the athletics track. But were the heroes victorious or defeated?

110. Joseph Guillemot of France was up against the great Paavo Nurmi in the 5,000 m of 1920 – but Guillemot was lucky to be running at all. He'd been gassed during the First World War in 1918 and had only taken up running to help his burned lungs. **Victorious or Defeated?**

111. Nurmi himself was faced with a severe challenge at the 1924 Olympics. After winning the gold medal in the 1,500 m he was out on the track again, just one hour later, for the 5,000 m final. **Victorious or Defeated?**

112. Michael Johnson (USA) was the hot favourite to win the 200 m at the 1992 Olympics – and then, just 12 days before the opening ceremony, he contracted food poisoning. **Victorious or Defeated?**

113. In 1952, Emil Zatopek was leading in the 10,000 m race when he suddenly wobbled, gasped and generally began to slow down. Soon the rest of the field had caught him up. **Victorious or Defeated?**

114. Dieudonne Kwizera had tried to get to the Olympics in both 1988 and 1992, but had not been allowed because his country, Burundi, didn't have an official Olympics organization. Finally, after putting lots of time and his own money into forming a committee, Kwizera made it on to the track for the 1,500 m in 1996. **Victorious or Defeated?**

115. In 1996, Venuste Niyangabo of Burundi had deliberately given up his place in the 1,500 m so that his teammate Kwizera could fulfil his ambition. Instead, Niyangabo competed in the 5,000 m – a distance he'd run only twice before. **Victorious or Defeated?**

Answers:

110. Victorious. Guillemot won gold, inflicting a rare defeat on Nurmi who said after the race: "Joseph ran with God at his side."

111. Victorious. Yes, just an hour after winning the 1,500 m Nurmi took gold in the 5,000 m too – in an Olympic-record time!

112. Defeated. Miserable Michael didn't recover quickly enough and was knocked out in the semi-finals (although he did win a gold medal with the USA 4 x 400 m relay team). He made up for it, though. After winning 54 straight finals at 400 m he won the 1996 race by 10 m – the biggest winning margin in Olympic history. Three days later, he won the 200 m in a world-record time, and broke the world 200 m record. In 2000, he became the first-ever athlete to retain the 400 m title.

113. Victorious. Zatopek was famous for gamesmanship and he was only pretending. When the others caught up, he immediately raced off again to win the gold – and beat the world record by 42 seconds!

114. Defeated. Kwizera came nowhere – but when he finished he kissed the track in gratitude.

115. Victorious. Niyangabo nipped in to cause a major surprise and get the reward his generosity deserved.

Did you know?

The famous name of Nurmi featured amongst the gold medallists in 1936, too – for equestrianism. German rider Ludwig Stubbendorf's horse had been given the name of the star athlete.

IT LOOKS LIKE THIS RACE IS GOING TO BE RUN AT A GALLOP

Oops, scoops and bloops

Once upon a time, athletes were only expected to run or jump or throw. They would let their performances do the talking for them. All that's changed and now we're bombarded with quotes...

THE WINNER OF THE 100 QUOTES RACE IS...

So here's a quiz about quotes in which you must work out what was really said by finding homes for these snippets:

backside, be the best, darns socks, don't bother, hero to zero, if I die here I die here, Mickey Mouse, shifter, take away, too old

Sometimes athletes say things and later wish they'd kept their mouths shut. Like these blunders below. Replace the word OOPS! by what was really said.

116. Said USA's star middle-distance runner Mary Decker Slaney: "What's the use of doing something if you don't try to OOPS!?"

117. Britain's 1,500 m runner, Steve Ovett, voicing his opinion of the ten-event decathlon in 1980, described it as: "Nine OOPS! events and a 1,500 metres."

118. Kenya's Kipchoge Keino explaining in 1968 why he was planning to run dangerously fast in the 1,500 m final: "This is the race of my life. OOPS!"

119. When the Dutch mother-of-two Fanny Blankers-Koen turned up at the London Olympics in 1948, the British team manager, Jack Crump, said: "She's OOPS! to win anything."

120. Said Canada's sprinter Ben Johnson when asked before the 1988 Games whether he'd prefer to win a gold medal or break the world record: "The gold medal. It's something they can't OOPS!"

Every newspaper tries to get a scoop by either printing a quote – or making something up. Replace SCOOP! by what was really printed:

121. After Ben Johnson's disqualification "From SCOOP! in 9.79 seconds."

122. After her successes in 1948 the *Daily Graphic* newspaper printed a profile of Dutch superstar Fanny Blankers-Koen: "She is an expert cook and SCOOP! with artistry."

123. When Ethopia's Miruts Yifter won both the 5,000 and 10,000 m golds in 1980, the papers nicknamed him: "Yifter the SCOOP."

And, finally, some things are said which TV companies have to cover with a "bloop" before the programme can go out. Replace "BLOOP" in this pair of bad-tempered quotes from those who didn't win...

124. Mary Decker Slaney to Zola Budd, when the latter asked how she was after the two had collided in 1984: "BLOOP!"

125. USA sprinter Jackson Scholz, 100 m silver medallist in 1924, when asked years later for his memories of the man who'd beaten him, Britain's Harold Abrahams: "I remember his BLOOP!"

Answers:

116. be the best. Sadly Decker Slaney never proved it at an Olympics. She was injured in 1976, the USA boycotted the Games in Moscow in 1980 and when miserable Mary finally got on the track in 1984 she was in a collision and didn't finish the race.

117. Mickey Mouse. Embarassing, as the 1980 decathlon was won by his British teammate, Daley Thompson.

118. If I die here, I die here. Was Kipchoge kidding? Whether he was or not, he won the gold and lived to tell the tale.

119. too old. Blankers-Koen was 30. Crump was crazy. Flying Fanny won four gold medals in the 100 m, 200 m, 80 m hurdles and 4 x 100 m relay.

120. take away. But they did. Two days after Johnson broke the world record and won gold in the 100 m, he was found guilty of drug taking. He was stripped of both medal and record.

121. hero to zero. Referring to Johnson's world-record time, this graffito turned up on a wall in the athlete's village before finding its way into the papers.

122. darns socks. It gushed on: "Her greatest love next to racing is housework!"

123. Shifter. He'd ended both races with sizzling sprints.

124. Don't bother. Budd should have been grateful; at least Decker didn't deck her!

125. backside. Except that Scholz didn't say "backside".

HAVING A FIELD DAY

...And that doesn't mean an Olympic event that has a midfield (like football) or an outfield (like baseball).

Field events at the Olympic Games involve throwing things, like the javelin and discus, and jumping as far or as high as possible (but not at the same time!). They are lumped together with track events and called *Athletics*.

Field events were amongst the competitions first seen in the ancient Olympics. Events like javelin-throwing came straight from the battlefield (so if you think that's why they're called "field events" you could have a point, ho-ho!).

Five field firsts

There have been plenty of notable firsts at the modern Games too. See if you can pick the winners from this field...

126. Legend has it that the modern discus evolved from something first thrown at the earliest of the ancient Olympics. Was it:

127. Triple-jump winner James Brendan Connolly's leap of 13.71 m was enough to make him the first modern Olympic – what?
a) Field-event champion.
b) Champion from the USA.
c) Champion in any event.

128. In 1968, Dick Fosbury (USA) became the first person to flop in his event – which was what?
a) The high jump.
b) The javelin.
c) The pole vault.

129. In 1988, Russian pole vaulter Sergei Bubka won a gold medal and claimed an Olympic record for his first – what?
a) His first clear jump in the competition.
b) His first try at the pole vault.
c) The first time the pole vault had appeared at the Olympics.

130. Harold Osborn was the first athlete to win the high jump by – doing what?

RUNNING IN WITH HIS EYES SHUT

WEARING TROUSERS TO SAVE HIS KNEES

USING HIS HANDS TO PREVENT A FALL

Answers:
126. b) This is known because of a boulder that has survived to this day. It's inscribed: "Bubon, son of Pholos, threw me over his head using one hand." Apart from a difference in shape, there's the small matter of weight, too. A modern men's discus weighs 2 kg; Bubon's boulder weighed in at 143.5 kg!
127. c) Connolly's event was the first competition decided at the 1896 Olympics – which means he was **a)** and **b)** as well. It was a triple victory in more ways than one!
128. a) Fosbury invented the head-first, go-over-backwards style that all high-jumpers use today – and won gold. His technique was immediately dubbed "the Fosbury Flop".

Having a field day

129. a) Sergei was so supreme in his event that, before it began, newspaper advertisements said: "air-traffic control have been alerted!" He didn't even bother to jump until virtually all the other competitors had dropped out – and then failed with his first two attempts. His one successful vault was enough to win him the gold medal.

130. c) The fall in question was that of the bar he was trying to clear! This was in 1924, when the high-jump bar balanced on pegs sticking out of the back of the side posts. Osborn had perfected a (then, quite legal) technique of pressing the bar against the nearest post so that it didn't fall off. After this, the practice was outlawed and the design of the posts changed to make sure it couldn't happen again.

Jesse, Luz – and angry Adolf

The 1936 Olympics took place in Germany's capital, Berlin. This section describes what happened in one particular event. Using the words below, fill in the gaps to complete the moving story.

100, black, favourite, long, marker, no-jumps, qualified, races, long, record, relay, second, three, world

Jesse Owens was a fantastic athlete. In one afternoon at a meeting in the USA, he had broken **(131.)** .... world records and equalled a fourth. He travelled to the 1936 Olympics as a hot **(132.)** .... to win gold medals in each of his events: the **(133.)** .... metres, the 200 metres and the **(134.)** .... jump. But Adolf Hitler, the German dictator, was desperate to use the Olympic Games to prove his theory that some **(135.)** .... were superior to others. He'd made it clear to one of his country's athletes, long-jumper Luz **(136.)** .... that he had to beat Jesse Owens. This wasn't because Owens was the holder of the **(137.)** .... record, but simply because he was **(138.)** .... But when the qualifying event began, Owens hit trouble. His first two attempts were **(139.)** .... One more and he would be eliminated. That was when Luz told Owens that his **(140.)** .... was too far forward. Owens moved it back – and **(141.)** .... for the final. There he not only won the gold medal, but broke the world **(142.)** .... again. As for Luz Long, he came **(143.)** .... Jesse Owens went on to win his three individual gold medals – plus a fourth when USA won the 100 metres **(144.)** ....

Answers:
131. three
132. favourite
133. 100
134. long
135. races
136. Long
137. world
138. black
139. no-jumps
140. marker
141. qualified
142. record
143. second
144. relay

JESSE OWENS

Did you know?

After the 1936 Olympics were over...

• *Luz Long died fighting bravely in the Second World War, which Hitler started; Hitler committed suicide rather than be captured.*

• *Jesse Owens carried on running and spent a lot of his time arranging sports meetings for under-privileged children. He died in 1980, aged 66.*

• *In 1984, the street leading to the Olympic Stadium in Berlin was renamed Jesse Owens Strasse. There are no streets in Germany named after Adolf Hitler.*

Dafter, lower, straighter

Sometimes you'd be forgiven for thinking that the Olympic motto of *Faster, Higher, Stronger* should be changed for the field events. Here's a selection of incidents to illustrate why. Pick the correct answer – if you can!

145. In 1924, Robert LeGendre (USA) broke the world record for the long jump – but didn't win the gold medal. Why not?
a) He wasn't in the long-jump competition.
b) Another jumper also broke the world record, but by more.
c) He was disqualified for having springs on his heels.

146. Natasa Urbancic of Yugoslavia pulled out all the stops with her final throw in the 1972 women's javelin final – and just missed … what?

A PIGEON

A PHOTOGRAPHER

A MEDAL

147. Robert Garrett (USA), the reigning Olympic champion, launched his discus in spectacular fashion in 1900. Where?
a) Out of the stadium.
b) Into the crowd.
c) Back over his head.

148. Sweden's William Pettersson spent the whole of his event in 1920 jumping about with something in his shoe. What was it?
a) A nail.
b) A stone.
c) A coin.

149. Another group of athletes had trouble with their feet in 1908. A team from Great Britain successfully competed in – what sort of footwear?

POLICEMEN'S BOOTS   DIVING BOOTS   WELLINGTON BOOTS

150. Harold Abrahams had been selected to compete for Britain in the 1924 long jump – but he wanted to concentrate on his main event, the 100 m. So artful Abrahams put pen to paper and wrote – what?

a) A sick note.

b) A protest letter.

c) A ransom note.

151. Reigning Olympic women's javelin champion Elvira Ozolina (Soviet Union) showed her feelings after the 1964 event was over. She went out – to do what?

a) Have a slap-up meal.

b) Buy a new dress.

c) Have her hair done.

152. Another javelin-thrower, Sue Platt of Great Britain, reacted in a different way to her performance in the 1960 competition. What did she do?

a) Jump for joy.

b) Sing the national anthem.

c) Dance the can-can.

153. After qualifying for the 1900 long-jump final, Myer Prinstein (USA) managed to get second place in a unique way – how?

BY NOT JUMPING
AT ALL

BY HOPPING DOWN
THE RUNWAY

BY LANDING ON
HIS HANDS

154. In 1912, Finland's Armas Taipale did it with his right and with his left, winning gold both times. Patrick McDonald (USA), though, didn't do as well and had to settle for gold and silver. What were they using?

a) Their eyes.

b) Their hands.

c) Their feet.

155. Jules Noel, from France, had really bad luck in the 1932 discus final. He'd just let go the furthest throw of the competition only to be told to take it again. Why?

a) The judges hadn't been watching.

b) He'd used a ladies' discus.

c) His throw had landed in the high-jump pit.

Answers:
145. a) LeGendre was competing in the five-event pentathlon. He came third overall even though William Hubbard (USA) made a long-jump leap that was 32 cm shorter.

146. b) The photographer wasn't watching, and almost got a really close close-up of a zooming javelin. Answer **c)** also applies; Natasa finished fifth.

147. b) Not once, not twice, but with all three throws!

148. c) He'd found it just before the long-jump final and put it in his shoe for luck. When he won, Pettersson was head (and tails) over heels with joy!

149. a) The victorious British tug-of-war team were all London policemen. Their everyday working boots helped them to get a really firm grip on the gold!

150. b) The letter (which he didn't sign) said how stupid it was to pick him for the long jump, when he should be concentrating on the 100 m. Abrahams then showed it to the people in charge of team selection and suggested they left him out. They did – and hurtling Harold went on to win the 100 m.

151. c) Not for a glam new look, though. Ozolina had come fifth and was so disgusted with herself that she went out and had her head shaved.

152. a) Unfortunately, it was during the competition. Plonker Platt, after launching a throw good enough to put her in second place, jumped for joy so much that she stepped over the line throwers mustn't cross and the throw was disallowed. Try as she might sad Sue couldn't produce another one as good, and ended up in fourth spot.

153. a) Prinstein wouldn't take part because the final round was held on a Sunday. But in 1900 qualifying round jumps counted – and his qualifying leap won him second place.

154. b) At the 1912 Olympics, there were both single- and two-handed versions of the shot, discus and javelin competitions (two-handed meant throwing first with one hand, then the other, and adding together the distances). Taipale won gold in both for the discus; McDonald won gold for single-handed shot throwing but could only manage silver in the two-handed competition.

155. a) They'd all been watching (and discus-ing!) an obviously more interesting pole-vault competition. Noel's extra throw was nothing like as good and he only ended up in fourth place.

Quirky quotes

You've just finished your race and you're exhausted. All you want to do is crawl off the track and back to the changing room. What happens instead? A reporter starts asking you questions! So it wouldn't be surprising if you got all your words mixed up – like in the five quotes below. Put the underlined words back into the speakers' mouths the way they really came out!

156. Jesse Owens, triple Olympic champion in 1936: "I let my <u>athlete</u> spend as little time on the <u>world</u> as possible."

157. Fatima Whitbread, powerful British woman javelin thrower, who came third in 1984 and second in 1988: "People think of me as the incredible <u>King</u>."

158. Tessa Sanderson, from Britain, who won the gold for the javelin in 1984 after failing to qualify in 1980: "In 1980 I was frightened to death of the <u>ground</u> but I took it like a <u>hulk</u> and came back."

159. King Gustav of Sweden, presenting the gold medal to decathlete Jim Thorpe (USA) in 1912: "Sir, you are the greatest <u>feet</u> in the <u>competition</u>."

160. Jim Thorpe's reply: "Thanks, <u>man</u>."

Answers:

156. "I let my <u>feet</u> spend as little time on the <u>ground</u> as possible," was Owens' explanation of how he ran so fast down the long-jump runway and track.

157. "People think of me as the incredible <u>hulk</u>," said muscle-girl Fatima.

158. "In 1980 I was frightened to death of the <u>competition</u> but I took it like a <u>man</u> and came back." Tessa Sanderson, getting a little confused.

159. "Sir, you are the greatest <u>athlete</u> in the <u>world</u>." He was right, too. The 1912 Games included a five-event pentathlon and a ten-event decathlon. Jim Thorpe had won them both! As if that wasn't enough, later in his career, genius Jim went on to play top American football and baseball.

160. "Thanks, <u>King</u>!" "Your Majesty," might have been better, but nobody could say that Thorpe was wrong!

A RIGHT FIGHT

The fighting sports – boxing, judo and wrestling – are an important part of the Olympic Games. Judo is a relatively new Olympic sport, but boxing and wrestling have been around since the ancient Olympics. In those days, the fighters didn't wear gloves. They didn't wear anything else, either. One of the rules at the ancient Games was that the athletes competed in the nude!

That rule no longer applies, but others do – like those for ensuring fair fights. It wouldn't be right if a skinny shrimp climbed into the ring and found himself being beaten up by a ten-tonne titanic. So to stop that happening, all the fighting sports divide competitors into different weight groups. That way, if they do get beaten up, at least it will be by somebody who weighs roughly the same as them.

Weigh to go!

Boxing has always used names for its weight groups. Not names like "Stanley" or "Wilhemina", but ones like "flyweight" (in which the descriptive part "fly" is used to say that a boxer in that weight group isn't very heavy at all!).

Here's the complete list of weight names – except that they've been written with clues instead of descriptive words. Can you work out what the actual names of the groups are?

161. Not dark, lift off the ground weight.
162. Winged creature of the order Diptera weight.
163. Small chicken weight.
164. Tickly thing weight.
165. Form of electromagnetic radiation weight.
166. Mucky wallow weight.
167. Bellybutton weight.
168. Not one or the other weight.
169. Weighs a lot weight.
170. Wonderful, dumb bodyguard weight.

Answers:
161. Light flyweight.
162. Flyweight.
163. Bantamweight.
164. Featherweight.
165. Lightweight.
166. Welterweight. (Boxing also has a wallow-in-ping-pong-balls weight — in other words, a light welterweight!)
167. Middleweight. (Boxing also has an illuminated-belly-button weight — yes, a light middleweight!)
168. Light heavyweight.
169. Heavyweight.
170. Super heavyweight.

Did you know?

Judo has its own silly names, like extra-lightweight, plus half-sizes in the lightweight, middleweight and heavyweight categories.

LOOK—I TOLD YOU I WAS HALF-HEAVYWEIGHT!

Ancient and modern

Boxing and wrestling are both sports that featured in the ancient Games. But surely things have changed since then? You don't find the same things happening in the modern Olympics, do you?

Here's where you discover whether boxing is foxing or wrestling too testing. Decide whether the incidents described in this list apply to the ancient Games or the modern Olympics.

171. A wrestling bout once lasted for 11 hours and 40 minutes. **Ancient or Modern?**

172. A dead boxer was declared the winner of his bout. **Ancient or Modern?**

173. After a boxer surprisingly won his bout, a number of judges were sacked. **Ancient or Modern?**

174. A boxer was found guilty of bribing an official, but was still allowed to remain the winner. **Ancient or Modern?**

175. This champion boxer won a team contest with three other men – and it was fought out in the middle of winter! **Ancient or Modern?**

176. A wrestler would signal the start of the entertainment by hitting a huge gong with a hammer. **Ancient or Modern?**

177. A boxer was declared the winner of his fight after his opponent's teeth marks were found on his bare chest. **Ancient or Modern?**

178. Another wrestler gained the upper hand in his bout by rubbing sand in his opponent's eyes. **Ancient or Modern?**

179. Six wins in a row becomes the record for an Olympic wrestling champion. **Ancient or Modern?**

180. A man with a slave's name became the most famous Olympic boxer of his time. **Ancient or Modern?**

Answers:

171. Modern. It happened in 1912, in a bout won by Martin Klein of Russia against Alfred Asikainen of Finland. Klein was so exhausted afterwards, he couldn't fight for the gold medal and had to accept silver.

172. Ancient. The rule was that if a fighter was killed then he'd be declared the winner, and his opponent banished from all future Olympics.

173. Modern. In 1988 in Seoul, a suspiciously high number of Korean boxers had scored wins. The suspensions came after local boxer, Park Si-Hun, was judged to have beaten Roy Jones (USA). Jones was later awarded a cup as the best boxer in the Games!

174. Ancient. It was a boxer named Eupolus, who bribed three opponents to let him win at the Games in 388 BC. That was the rule. Although bribery was punishable by a flogging, a fine or a ban from future Olympics (or all three!) the cheat still prospered by being allowed to remain the winner.

175. Modern. The boxer was Ed Eagan (USA), light-heavyweight winner in 1920. Twelve years later, in 1932, Eagan was a member of the USA's winning four-man bob team at the Winter Games in Lake Placid – making him the first man to win both Summer and Winter Olympic gold medals.

176. Modern. Kenneth Richmond (Great Britain), who won a heavyweight wrestling bronze medal in 1952, became even more well known as the muscle man who did the gong-bashing at the start of films made by the Rank Organisation.

THEY WANTED A BIG NAME TO DRUM UP BUSINESS

177. Modern. It happened in 1924 to the middleweight champion, Great Britain's Harry Mallin. After losing his bout against Roger Brousse of France, Mallin showed the judges his chest. They agreed that Brousse had bitten the Briton and he was disqualified.

178. Ancient. Nowadays, wrestling bouts take place on mats; rubbing one of those into your opponent's eyes isn't so easy!

I CAN RUB HIS EYES INTO THE MAT, THOUGH!

179. Ancient. The record-holder was called Milo of Croton. He was reputed to be so strong that he could lift an ox!

I WAS HAVING LUNCH!

180. Modern. Cassius Clay (USA) was the Olympic light-heavyweight champion in 1960. Saying that his name was inherited from a slave ancestor, he later changed it – and, as Muhammad Ali, became the most famous boxer ever.

Did you know?

Muhammad Ali lost and regained the world heavyweight boxing title three times, once after having it taken away from him for refusing to join the US Army. By the time the Olympics came to Atlanta in 1996, though, all was forgiven. Muhammad Ali was given the honour of helping to light the Olympic flame.

Fighting talk

Judo and tae kwon do are the oldest *newest* Olympic fighting sports! Judo only made its first Olympic appearance in 1964, even though the word ju-do is found in Chinese writings of the first century. The Korean martial art of tae kwon do, which didn't become an Olympic event until 2000, is even older – dating back to 50 BC!

181. What does "judo" mean?
a) The strong way.
b) The quick way.
c) The gentle way.

182. What does "tae kwon do" mean?
a) The way of hands and feet.
b) The way of hands and eyes.
c) The way of eyes and feet.

Considering that they're supposed to be serene sports, judo and tae kwon do come with loads of gruesome talk! Do these scary seven terms apply to judo, tae kwon do ... or are they invented?

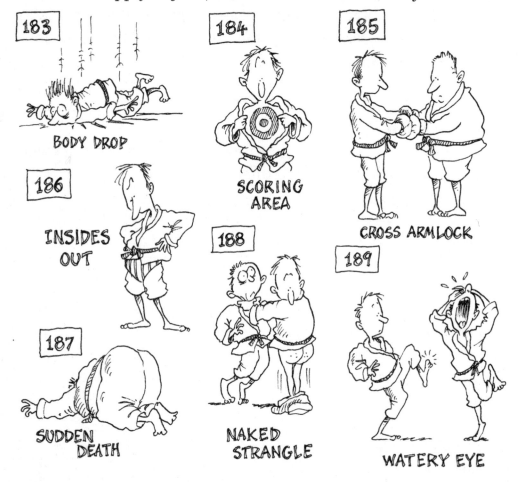

183

BODY DROP

184

SCORING AREA

185

CROSS ARMLOCK

186

INSIDES OUT

188

187

SUDDEN DEATH

NAKED STRANGLE

189

WATERY EYE

Answers:

183. Judo – it's a move in which a judoka (that's a judo contestant) throws his or her opponent over their outstretched leg.

184. Tae kwon do – the area of an opponent's face or body which a fighter is allowed to punch or kick to score a point.

185. Judo – in this, the poor victim finds a leg around his neck and an arm being stretched at the same time.

186. Invented

187. Tae kwon do – no, it's not as bad as it sounds. If a three-round Olympic final ends in a tie, the two fighters go into a "sudden death" fourth round, with the first to score a point being declared the winner.

188. Judo – a simple hold in which judokas choke their opponents by putting an arm round their neck from behind.

189. Invented

Did you know?
Fighters at the ancient Games got themselves fit by breaking rocks with a pick.

WHAT'S GOING ON?

HE'S BREAKING ROCKS. I'M PICKING 'EM!

SNATCHES AND SPLITS

Two sports that have been part of the Olympics since 1896 are weightlifting and gymnastics. You might think they're very different, but they've got a lot in common – and it's not simply that you can stay out of the rain when you watch them. Both require competitors to lift things. In weightlifting, it's a thing called a barbell, which has round heavy discs at each end; in gymnastics, the weight you have to swing over and around bits of equipment is yourself.

I feel odd

Here are some trios of wicked weightlifting facts – except that in each case only two are true. Find the odd one out.

190. Weightlifting in the 1896 Games had competitions for:
a) Two-arm lifts.
b) One-arm lifts.
c) No-arm lifts.

191. The weightlifting methods now used are called:
a) Snatch.
b) Grab.
c) Clean and jerk.

192. Lifting a weight above your head isn't enough. For any lift to be accepted by the judges, weightlifters also have to:

BE STANDING STILL

HAVE ONE LEG FORWARD AND THE OTHER BACK

HAVE THE WEIGHT STEADY

193. The animals which compare most closely to the heaviest weights ever lifted at the Olympics are:

And finally, a quartet of trios in which you have to find the correct answer from the three given…

194. Competitors in weightlifting are themselves grouped by weight. The lowest weight group for men is:
a) 48 kg.
b) 56 kg.
c) 64 kg.

195. If two lifters manage to lift exactly the same weight, which of the two is declared the winner?
a) The lighter.
b) The heavier.
c) Neither of them.

196. Women's weightlifting events were first included in the Olympics in:
a) 1896.
b) 1960.
c) 2000.

197. The lowest weight group for women is:
a) 48 kg.
b) 56 kg.
c) 64 kg.

Answers:

190. c) – though the one-arm lifting event was quickly thrown out!

191. b) In the "snatch", the lifter brings the bar to head height in one move. The "clean and jerk" is done in two stages: first to shoulder level, in which the lifter squats, then to head height while the lifter stands up.

192. b) The lifter can only be in this position during their lift. If they don't then straighten up, the lift isn't allowed.

193. c) – it's far too light! Olympic competitions add together the total weight each lifter manages for both the snatch and the clean and jerk. At the Sydney 2000 Games, Hossein Rezazadeh lifted a total of 472.5 kg – roughly the weight of both a cow and a giraffe!

194. b) The 2000 champion at this weight, Halil Mutlu of Turkey, lifted 168 kg in the clean and jerk – three times his own body weight.

195. a) – because he/she has lifted more times their own body weight they're assumed to be stronger, even though they're not. Geddit?

196. c) – yes, they had to weight all that time!

197. a) The 2000 champion at this weight, Isabela Dragneva of Bulgaria, lifted 105 kg in the clean and jerk – two and a half times her own body weight.

Weight for it!

Weightlifting events have their fair share of drama, with competitors and spectators alike wondering what's going to happen next. Work out what *did* happen next on these occasions…

198. Charles Vinci (USA) found himself with a weight problem in 1956. With just 15 minutes to go before the weigh-in, chubby Charles checked and found he was 200 grams too heavy! What happened next?

199. In 1996, Ronny Weller of Germany had lifted a world-record total of 455 kg. Russian Andrey Chemerkin then stepped up for his final lift of the competition. What happened to Weller next?

200. Harold Sakata (USA), won a silver medal for weightlifting in 1948. What famously happened to him next? (Quite a lot next – like, 16 years later).

a) He did a dance.

b) He threw his hat in the air.

c) He sang a song.

In the gym

If any athletes have taken the Olympic motto to heart, it's those who compete in the gymnastics events. They try to go higher, faster and stronger all at the same time! There are three events:

• artistic gymnastics, in which gymnasts do things on bits of equipment like beams, bars and pommel horses

• rhythmic gymnastics, in which competitors do things with bits of equipment, like ribbons, clubs and hoops

• trampolining, in which gymnasts do moves and bounce at the same time.

There are a mind-bending number of names for the body-

bending movements that gymnasts perform. But which of the following are real gymnastic moves and which aren't?

201. Cartwheel
202. Cat leap

203. Cross
204. Crunch
205. Double stagger
206. Flic-flac
207. Hitler

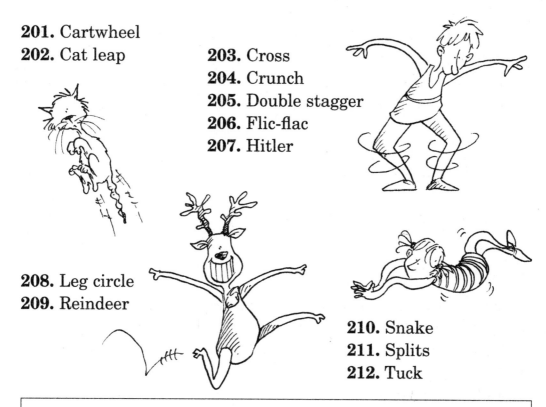

208. Leg circle
209. Reindeer

210. Snake
211. Splits
212. Tuck

Answers:

201. YES. A cartwheel is (according to the official Olympics description) "an acrobatic sideways roll with arms and legs extended". To you and me it's what you do when you're showing off in the playground!

202. YES. A cat leap means taking off from one foot, raising one knee then the other. Gymnasts score well if they do this purrfectly.

203. YES. Artistic gymnasts make a cross position on the "rings" equipment – two rings hung from the roof. They have to stretch their arms sideways and hold themselves up straight, making a cross shape (and they get really cross if they can't do it).

204. NO. A crunch is an exercise movement for strengthening your stomach muscles.

205. NO – not quite. A double stag is a move in rhythmic gymnastics, though, with the legs split and both knees bent, while the back's kept straight. The aim is to look like a stag's antlers.

206. YES. With a flic-flac jump, the gymnast takes off from one or two feet, jumps backwards onto the hands and lands on the feet.

207. NO – but an *Adolph* is a trampoline move! It's a front somersault with three-and-a-half twists.

208. YES. It's an artistic move on a pommel horse. You keep your legs together and swing them in a full circle around the horse, lifting each hand in turn to let the legs pass.

209. NO – but a *Rudolph* is! On the trampoline, it's a front somersault with one-and-a-half twists.

210. YES. It's a move rhythmic gymnasts perform using a stick and ribbon. By waggling the stick in the right way they produce a rippling movement of the ribbon that looks like a snake slithering through the air.

211. YES. It's a position where one leg points forward and the other backward, at right angles to the body.

212. YES – but a gymnastic tuck is nothing to do with nibbling chocolate between goes. It's a move in which your knees and hips are bent and drawn into your chest, while your body is folded at the waist.

The flexible five

Use the clues to match these five golden gymnasts to their achievements.

213 RAYMOND BASS (USA)
CLUE: DIDN'T TIE HIMSELF IN KNOTS.

214 NADIA COMANECI (ROMANIA)
CLUE: A PERFECT PERFORMER.

215 LARISSA LATYNINA
CLUE: NEEDED A BIG CHEST.

216 CARL SCHUHMANN (GERMANY)
CLUE: FLEXIBLE FIGHTER.

217 KERRI STRUG (USA)
CLUE: STRUG WAS STRUGGLING.

OOOPS!

A PERFORMED A FINAL VAULT WITH A TWISTED ANKLE TO HELP HER TEAM TO A 1996 GOLD.

B IN 1932, WON THE LAST OLYMPIC ROPE-CLIMBING EVENT.

D IN 1976, THE FIRST GYMNAST TO SCORE A PERFECT TEN DURING AN EVENT.

C WAS A GYMNASTICS CHAMPION IN 1896 — AND ALSO A CHAMPION IN WRESTLING.

E WINNER OF NINE GOLD MEDALS IN THREE OLYMPICS.

FOUL!

Answers:

213. b) Raymond Bass won the final 10 m rope-climbing gold medal in a time of 6.7 seconds! When it came to climbing, Raymond knew the ropes!

214. d) Comaneci did this seven times on her way to three gold medals. She was 14 at the time, having been training since she was six years old.

215. e) Lithe Larissa's three Olympic appearances in 1956, 1960 and 1964, left her with 18 medals all told.

216. c) At the 1896 Games, sharp-moving Schuhmann won the horse-vaulting title and the wrestling.

217. a) Kerri Strug had twisted her ankle during her first vault and wouldn't have jumped again but for thinking (mistakenly as it turned out) that her USA team needed the points to win team gold. Courageous Kerry, ankle swathed in bandages, had to be carried to the podium by her coach to get her medal. Aah!

Finally, for all those of you who fancy being a gymnastics champion, a quick quote question:

218. Nadia Comaneci, golden girl of the 1976 Games, explained the reason for her success by saying: "I was ...., that's all," What's the missing word?
a) Gifted.
b) Lucky.
c) Grateful.
d) Pretty.

Answer:
218. a) Gifted, yes. Modest, no.

Did you know?
In the early years of the Olympics, the gymnastics events weren't held in warm and cosy indoor arenas. They took place outdoors – in the grassy middle of the athletics track.

ROUND BUT NOT ROUNDERS

That favourite school game, rounders, hasn't officially been added to the list of Olympic ball events, but if you get a chance to watch a game of softball you'll see that it's really there under another name.

Others you won't find however hard you look. Cricket, rugby and golf may be popular, but they've all been thrown out of the Olympics at one time or another.

WHY DON'T YOU GO IN FOR WEIGHTLIFTING INSTEAD?

Some, like snooker, have *never* been on the programme. Even so, there's plenty of ball action to be found all around – as you'll see if you've got enough bounce to roll your way through this section.

True ... or bal-derdash?

"Balderdash" isn't a word that's used much nowadays. Well, it's time to change all that because balderdash means "nonsense" – which makes it a perfect word for this quiz. Here are some Olympic ball game incidents. Can you sort out the truth from the balderdash?

219. In 1932, India won the gold medal for field hockey, with the USA taking the bronze – but there really wasn't much to choose between the two teams. **Truth or Balderdash?**

220. Baseball was only introduced as an Olympic sport in 1936 after being a demonstration event in 1912. **Truth or Balderdash?**

221. After fielding a weak team in 1992 and only coming fourth behind gold-medallists Cuba, USA put out their strongest baseball team at Atlanta in 1996 and wiped the floor with everybody. **Truth or Balderdash?**

222. Wimbledon champion André Agassi won the Olympic men's singles tennis title in 1996, following his father who'd done the same in 1948 and 1952. **Truth or Balderdash?**

223. Whiff-whaff became an Olympic ball sport in 1988. **Truth or Balderdash?**

224. A 1976 Olympic volleyball match between Canada and Czechoslovakia was halted because the crowd all stood up to watch. **Truth or Balderdash?**

225. USA won the first Olympic football title in 1996. **Truth or Balderdash?**

226. Women footballers at the Olympics can't be older than 23 and men can't be younger than 16. **Truth or Balderdash?**

227. At the Olympics, the USA have dominated a men's ball game that originally needed a helper on a ladder. **Truth or Balderdash?**

228. When the USA suffered their first defeat at this sport in 1972, time stood still. **Truth or Balderdash?**

Answers:

219. Balderdash. In their group match, India beat USA 24-1. They won Olympic gold every Games until 1960.

220. Balderdash. Baseball had been a demonstration sport a record six times – in 1912, 1936, 1956, 1964, 1984 and 1988 – before finally being accepted as a regular Olympic sport in 1992.

221. Balderdash. Cuba won again, Japan took silver and USA bronze. USA finally won gold at their third attempt in 2000, beating Cuba in the final.

222. Balderdash. Mr Agassi Senior couldn't have played Olympic tennis in 1948 and 1952 because the sport was dropped from the Olympics in 1924, only returning in 1988.

André's dad did compete in 1948 and 1952, though, as a boxer, for his country – Iran.

223. Truth. "Whiff-whaff" was one of the names by which table tennis was known in England in the 1890s.

224. Truth. Because they weren't watching the volleyball. They'd got to their feet because members of the Royal Family had just turned up.

225. Truth – but we're talking *women's* football here, which didn't reach the Olympics until 1996. Norway won the title in 2000, beating USA in the final.

226. Balderdash – it's the other way round. Men can be professionals but, apart from three permitted over-age players, they have to be under 23; women can be any age at all, so long as they're at least 16.

227. Truth. The game is basketball, which the USA won every year from its introduction in 1936 to their first defeat by Russia in 1972. When invented in 1891, peach baskets on poles were used as goalposts and a helper had to climb a ladder to retrieve the ball whenever a point was scored!

228. Truth – kind of. In the 1972 basketball final the USA was a point ahead of Russia with one second to go when the judges decided that the official clock was wrong. They had it put back by three seconds ... giving Russia enough time to score the winning basket.

Sorting for size

If you've been going through life thinking a ball is just a ball, then
think again! Every Olympic ball sport has its own rules about
what makes a proper ball. The material it has to be made from,
how high it must bounce, what it should weigh – they're all
important. Oh, yes – and size matters of course.

Sort these sports balls in order of their legal maximum size, from
the smallest ball upwards:

Baseball
Basketball
Football
Handball
Hockey ball
Softball
Table tennis ball
Tennis ball
Volleyball
Water polo ball

Answers:

229. Table tennis ball, maximum diameter 3.82 cm – and it must be made of celluloid or some other plastic.

230. Hockey ball, 5.00 cm – and it must be hard!

231. Tennis ball, 6.67 cm – and it must be yellow or white.

232. Baseball, 6.99 cm – with a cork centre and two strips of horsehide stitched together.

233. Softball, 9.80 cm – made like a baseball, only softer.

234. Handball, 19.10 cm – and it must have a leather casing.

235. Volleyball, 21.32 cm – and it can't be multi-coloured.

236. Football, 22.28 cm – and it must weigh 410–450 g at the start of the match (including advertisements and all the other pretty pictures).

237. Water polo ball, 22.60 cm – and it must be, get ready … waterproof!

238. Basketball, 24.82 cm – and it should bounce between 1.2 and 1.4 metres if dropped onto a solid wooden floor from a height of 1.8 metres.

Pretty technical stuff, eh? And you thought balls were just round objects!

Did you know?

There's one Olympic racquet sport that doesn't use a whole ball – it uses a ball with a hole in it. Goose feathers are then stuck in the hole and the whole thing renamed a shuttlecock. Yes, we're talking about badminton, which only became an Olympic sport in 1992.

WATCH OUT. THEY'VE INVENTED A NEW GAME!

Going for "goal-d!"

The most popular ball sport in the world, Association Football (or soccer), was one of the first team sports included in the Olympic Games. The men's version made its debut in 1900 and – apart from 1932 in Los Angeles – has appeared at every Games since. Women's football was introduced in 1996.

So, who have been the star soccer squads in the Olympics? Find out with this football five-pack:

239. Three out of the first four Olympic football titles were won by which country?
a) Belgium.
b) Great Britain.
c) Canada.

240. Brazil, with five titles, has been the most successful country in the history of the professional football. But how many Olympic titles has Brazil won?
a) 0.
b) 1.
c) 5.

241. Hungary has won the Olympic title three times, on each occasion with a team made up mostly of – what?

COOKS

TEACHERS

SOLDIERS

242. Uruguay hosted, and won, the first-ever football World Cup in 1930. But how had Uruguay done in the 1928 Olympic Games?
a) They won gold.
b) They won silver.
c) They won bronze.

243. The same country won soccer medals in 1904, 1996 and 2000. Which country was it?
a) USA.
b) Cameroon.
c) Norway.

Answers:

239. b) A combined Great Britain team won in 1900, 1908 and 1912. Canada (true!) won in 1904 and Belgium in 1920.

240. a) When it comes to the Olympics, Brazil has always drawn a blank.

241. c) The majority of the team was in the Hungarian army – which made them "amateur" footballers, even though they didn't do any soldiering and spent all their time playing!

YOU 'ORRIBLE LOSERS, YOU, GET PEELING THOSE POTATOES!

242. a) It was because they were reigning Olympic champions that Uruguay were chosen as the first World Cup hosts.

243. a) The USA men won silver in 1904 ... but the USA women won gold in 1996 and silver in 2000. What would Baron de Coubertin have said?

RIDING RIDDLES

The two main events at the Olympics that are devoted to riders and saddles are cycling and horse riding (known as equestrianism).

HORSES ARE NO GOOD FOR THE ROAD.

BIKES ARE NO GOOD FOR THE GARDEN.

Others events have had cycling or horse riding playing bit parts, though.

244. What are they?
a) Triathlon.
b) Modern pentathlon.
c) Gymnastics.
d) Athletics.

Answer:
244. All of them! a) Triathlon, introduced in 2000, involves cycling plus swimming and running. **b)** Modern pentathlon, first seen in 1912 involves horse riding plus shooting, fencing, swimming and running. **c)** In 1920, but never again, there was a vaulting event for horses. And ... **d)** Just once, in 1900, horses had their own Olympic high jump and long jump events!

Saddle up!

Horses have always been hard done by. The winners of the chariot race at the ancient Games didn't collect an award. Neither did the chariot-driver, for that matter – the laurel crown went to the horse's owner. And although it's now the rider who picks up the medals, the horse still leaves the arena empty-hoofed.

Is this fair? Try these questions to see how horses would get on if they were to compete against human athletes...

245. In 1900, the winning horse high jump was better than the winning human high jump. **True or False?**
246. The winning horse long jump that year was better than the winning human long jump. **True or False?**

> **Answers:**
> **245. False.** The horse, ridden by Dominique Gardères of France jumped 1.85 m but human Irving Baxter (USA) topped that with 1.90 m!
> **246. False.** The horse, ridden by C. van Langhendonck of Belgium leapt 6.10 m – only to be well out-jumped by Alvin Kraenzlein (USA) with 7.18 m.

247. Also in the 1900 human athletics, there was a standing long jump event, in which competitors didn't take a run up. That was won by Ray Ewry (USA) – and he out-jumped the horse too. **True or False?**

> **Answer:**
> **247. False.** Ewry's jump was just 3.21 m. (But could the horse have done better without a gallop-up?)

Pedal power

There have been cycling events of one kind or another in each Olympics from 1896 to the present day, though women didn't start competing in their own events until 1984.

Cycling events come in three types nowadays: road racing, track racing and mountain biking – and they have lots of strange cycling terms to go with them.

Use your own biking knowledge to match these words to their definitions:

248 HIGHSIDE		ⓐ THE LOWEST GEAR.
249 ROCK DODGE		ⓑ ORIGINAL TERM FOR MOUNTAIN BIKING.
250 SNAKEBITE		ⓒ TO STEER THE HANDLEBARS QUICKLY TO ONE SIDE TO AVOID SMALL ROAD HAZARDS.
251 CARVE		ⓓ BEING THROWN FROM THE BICYCLE.
252 CLUNKING		ⓔ FLAT TYRE.
253 GRANNY GEAR		ⓕ TO MAKE A GROOVE IN THE TRACK BY SPINNING THE BACK TYRE.

Answers:

248. d) In particular, falling off one way while your bike turns a corner the other way!

249. c) A hard trick, but a lot harder if you don't manage it!

250. e) One caused by hitting something (like the kerb) so hard that the inner tube is pinched against the wheel's rim.

251. f) Usually a dirt track, not the pavement!

252. b) From the early days of the sport when mountain bikes as you know them didn't exist and riders would just take everything possible off their bikes to make them lighter (mudguards, brakes) ... but not wheels) and clunk off across the countryside.

253. a) Because in this gear you need so little pedal power that even your granny could manage it!

Horse sense ... or bike brains?

Here are some real riding facts from the Olympics. But – are they connected to equestrian or cycling events? Do you have horse sense or bike brains? Select horse or cycle in each case.

254. This game of polo was a demonstration event at the 1908 Olympics. **Horse or Cycle?**

255. No medals were awarded in this 1932 team event because none of the teams had all their three riders complete the circuit. **Horse or Cycle?**

256. Lis Hartel of Denmark was an amazing and courageous woman. After suffering from polio, she won silver medals in her event in both 1952 and 1956. **Horse or Cycle?**

257. After suffering a badly broken arm, British competitor Virginia Holgate thought she'd never take part in her event again – until a vet cured her! **Horse or Cycle?**

258. This ride across country was introduced to the Olympics in 1996. **Horse or Cycle?**

259. There was a close finish in a 1936 event involving Robert Charpentier and Guy Lapebie (both from France). Charpentier was suspected of nobbling his rival by grabbing his shirt to slow him down. **Horse or Cycle?**

260. Although the 1956 Summer Games took place in Melbourne, Australia, these events were held in Stockholm. The cause? The stiff rules laid down by the Australian Government for checking parts were in working order. **Horse or Cycle?**

261. After HRH Princess Anne rode for Great Britain at the 1976 Olympics – and had the world's cameras trained on her every move – she said: "This **Horse or Cycle?** is just about the only one who doesn't know I'm royal!"

262. The oldest woman competitor to date is Lorna Johnstone, who took part in an event at the age of 70 years and 5 days. **Horse or Cycle?**

Answers:

254. Cycle. The demonstration sport was bicycle polo … but it never wheel-y caught on! Neither did horse-riding polo, for that matter, which was tossed out of the Olympics after 1936.

255. Horse. It happened in the showjumping, where the tough circuit prevented all the riders putting on a good show.

256. Horse. The illness had left Lis unable to move her legs from the knees down, so she had to be lifted on and off her horse. Her medals were won in the dressage event.

257. Horse. After a fall in 1976, Holgate's arm was broken in 23 places! Even when it had mended she couldn't ride properly. Then a vet studied her X-rays, gave her arm a good pull – and fixed it. A revitalized Virginia was able to saddle up and win a bronze medal in the 1984 Games.

258. Cycle. This was the year mountain biking joined the Olympics.

259. Cycle. A stewards' enquiry didn't change the result: Charpentier kept the gold medal.

260. Horse. The horses would have had to have been quarantined for six months.

261. Horse – of course!

262. Horse. Lively Lorna was in the dressage event.

THE FROZEN OLYMPICS

If there's one feature of the modern Olympics that would have left ancient Olympians cold, it's the Winter Games – they competed in the nude, remember!

The Winter Olympics are a completely modern invention. But how modern?

263. Did any of these events feature in the 1920 Olympic Games?
a) Figure skating.
b) Ice hockey.
c) Ski jumping.

> **Answer:**
> **263. a)** and **b)** Figure skating, in fact, had been in the Olympics since 1908.

As winter sports grew in popularity, it was decided to increase the number to include other events like ski jumping, speed skating and bobsledding. From 1924, there were two sets of Olympic Games – the Summer Games, which take place every four years, and the Winter Games which take place…

264. How often?
a) Every two years.
b) Every eight years.
c) Every four years.

Glacial and gone

When a city or town hosts the Winter Olympics, they're obviously hoping that they've thought of everything and missed nothing. It doesn't always work out that way, though. In this frozen five, the word MISSING plays a big part. Choose the missing item from these:

ice, skiers, snow, snow, trees

265. For the 1964 Winter Games in Innsbruck, Austrian troops had to be called in to deal with a problem of missing ....

266. The skiing course for the 1994 Games in Lillehammer, Norway, was designed so as to ensure that there wouldn't be too many missing ....

267. In 1980 there was plenty of white stuff on the ground in Lake Placid, USA, in spite of the fact that real .... was missing.

268. The bobsled course for the 1998 Games in Nagano, Japan, was designed so that nobody need worry about missing ....

269. In 1932, the 50 km skiing event wound through a lonely stretch of woods and led to the unusual problem of missing ....

Answers:

265. snow. Innsbruck had had its mildest winter for years and the snow on the course had all melted. Austrian troops went into the mountains and brought down 25,000 tons of it.

266. trees. The Norwegians showed their concern for the environment by ensuring that Olympic buildings would be used when the Games were over – and by chopping down as few trees as possible.

267. snow again. No troops were called in this time, though.

Instead the organizers spent $5 million (worth over $10 million today) on artificial snow. Unreal, or what!

268. ice. The bobsled course wasn't natural, but man-made. With computer-controlled coolant pipes beneath the surface, it was like a long refrigerator. All they had to do was fill it up with water and turn on the power!

269. skiers. The solitary stretch wasn't only closed to spectators – but also to race officials. When skiers weren't sure which way to go, they had nobody to ask. They just had to try and find their own way out!

Numbed numbers

The Olympics Quiz Book computer has got its digits in a twist and jumbled up the numbers in these frosty facts. Put the numbers back where they belong.

270. In 1924 at the first Winter Games in Chamonix, France, a bobsled team could number <u>110</u> men.

271. Canada skated away with the 1924 ice-hockey title, scoring <u>800</u> goals.

272. An extra ski-jump competition was introduced in 1964. Jumpers could now enjoy throwing themselves off a hill <u>11</u> metres high.

273. In 1936 at Garmisch-Partenkirchen, Germany, the reigning champions – Canada – were stunned when they lost their ice-hockey title to Great Britain – especially as the winning team included <u>90</u> players who didn't live in Britain!

274. Norwegian figure skater Sonja Henie came last in her event in the 1924 Games. Understandable really, considering she was <u>four or five</u> years old.

275. Olympic regulations say that for the downhill-skiing events, the start point of a course has to be <u>54</u> metres higher than the finish.

276. Gold medallists Jane Torvill and Christopher Dean, from Britain, made history in 1984 by receiving the maximum possible <u>eight</u> points from the judges for the "artistic impression" segment of their ice-dancing event.

Answers:

270. In 1924 a bobsled team could number <u>four or five</u> men. It was up to the team to decide.

271. Canada skated away with the 1924 ice-hockey title, scoring <u>110</u> goals – and conceding just three!

272. In 1964, jumpers could enjoy throwing themselves off a hill <u>90</u> metres high. This was called "the big hill" to differentiate it from "the small hill" competition which involved jumping from a mere 70 metres in the air.

273. The 1936 British team included <u>eight</u> players who didn't live in Britain. They'd been born in Britain (which meant that they could play for them) but lived and played their ice hockey in ... Canada, the country they beat in the final!

274. At the 1924 Games, Sonja Henie was <u>11</u> years old. She made up for it, though, going on to win the event three Games running in 1928, 1932 and 1936.

275. For the downhill-skiing events the start point of a course has to be <u>800</u> metres higher than the finish. This was a problem for Sarajevo, Yugoslavia, when the Winter Olympics were held there in 1984. They had to build a special high-rise start line to meet the rules.

276. Torvill and Dean received the maximum possible <u>54</u> points – six points from each of the nine judges.

Arctic 'appenings

There have been some strange events seen at the Winter Olympics – but were they all to do with proper Olympic winter sports events? Judge for yourself. Were each of the following to do with real events, or non-events?

277. In 1994, spectators at the Winter Games in Lillehammer, Norway, saw a number of sleds being pulled across ice by teams of four-legged animals. **Event or Non-Event?**

278. In 1932, spectators at the Winter Games in Lake Placid, USA, saw a number of sleds being pulled across ice by teams of four-legged animals. **Event or Non-Event?**

279. At Chamonix in 1924, Charles Granville Bruce was awarded a medal for mountain climbing. **Event or Non-Event?**

280. At the 1994 Winter Games, Marc Gagnon (Canada) won a bronze medal for doing something faster than anybody else. **Event or Non-Event?**

281. People with numbers on their back and big boots on their feet regularly took to the ice at the 1936 Winter Olympics. **Event or Non-Event?**

282. A boy/girl partnership named Hidy and Howdy featured heavily at Calgary, Canada in 1988. **Event or Non-Event?**

Answers:

277. Non-Event. The four-legged creatures were reindeer, and the spectators were watching a pageant during the opening ceremony.

278. Event. The four-legged creatures were dogs, and this was a dog-sled race. (As it was only included as a demonstration event, and has never been included as an official Olympic sport, **Non-Event** is a correct answer too!)

279. Non-Event. At the early Winter Games, honorary medals – called "Merits for Alpinism" – were awarded to people who'd done something in snowy mountains. Charles Granville Bruce got his for being the leader of a 1922 expedition that attempted (and failed) to climb Mount Everest.

280. Event. The 1 km short track skating event, to be exact. Heats were used to find the fastest skaters for an "A" final to decide gold and silver. The winner of a "B" final would get the bronze medal. Gagnon felt great when he won the "B" race, but turned into Mad Marc when he learned his time was faster than that of the gold and silver winners from the "A" final!

281. Event. But if you thought it was ice hockey, be honest and deduct a point. The people were the judges for the figure-skating competition who would take to the ice in order to get a close-up view of the skaters during a section in which they had to skate some compulsory exercises.

282. Non-Event, but they did turn up at most events. Hidy and Howdy were the Games' polar bear mascots.

YOU ALWAYS HAVE TO SHOW OFF!

Polar problems

Just because the Winter Olympics take place in cold weather doesn't mean that there aren't plenty of heated arguments – as this collection of polar problems shows. They weren't as described here, though, because their causes have been mixed up. Rearrange the underlined words to show the true picture.

283. In 1932, Finnish world champion speed skater Clas Thunberg refused to start with other competitors because <u>they were married</u>.

284. In 1964, slalom silver medallist Marielle Goitschel wanted to get her own back on the girl who'd won gold even though <u>she'd arranged for her to be beaten up</u>.

285. Many Austrian and Swiss competitors were banned from taking part in 1936 because <u>they weren't heavy enough</u>.

286. The 1952 four-man bobsled winners, Germany, only triumphed after realizing that <u>they were warming their runners before a race</u>.

287. Also in 1952, Ria and Paul Falk managed to combine wonderfully to win the pairs figure skating even though <u>they were hotel ski instructors</u>.

288. In 1968, three female East German competitors in the luge event (a luge is a kind of sliding tea-tray) were disqualified because <u>they were sisters</u>.

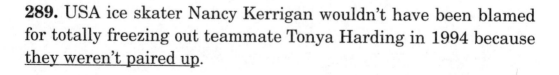

289. USA ice skater Nancy Kerrigan wouldn't have been blamed for totally freezing out teammate Tonya Harding in 1994 because <u>they weren't paired up</u>.

Answers:

283. Careful Clas refused to start with other competitors because <u>they weren't paired up</u>. The usual way of starting speed skating events was to send the skaters out in pairs to avoid collisions. When the organizers decided to scrap this and have a big scramble at the start Thunberg thumbed his nose at them and withdrew.

284. Marielle Goitschel wanted to get her own back on the girl who'd won gold even though <u>they were sisters</u>. Yes, it was her sister Christine who'd beaten her into second place. Marielle did it, too. In the giant slalom event she won gold – with Christine having to settle for silver.

285. Many Austrian and Swiss competitors were banned from taking part in 1936 because <u>they were hotel ski instructors</u>. Only amateurs were allowed to compete and because ski instructors were paid to teach gallumping guests, that ruled them out. It caused a holy hotel row because that was the job all the best skiers did when they weren't skiing.

286. Germany's four-man bob team only triumphed after realizing that <u>they weren't heavy enough</u>. Noticing how well heavyweight teams did in training runs, the Germans scrapped the two light squads they were going to enter and came up with one that was gargantuan enough to grab the gold.

287. Ria and Paul Falk managed to combine wonderfully to win the pairs figure skating even though <u>they were married</u>. (Or *because* they were married!)

288. Three female East German luge competitors were disqualified because <u>they were warming their runners before a race</u>. Why did this trick get such a frosty reception? Because it was designed to help them to a faster time by melting bits of ice that would otherwise stick to their runners and slow them down).

289. Nancy Kerrigan wouldn't have been blamed for totally freezing out Tonya Harding because <u>she'd arranged for her to be beaten up</u>. It had happened at that year's USA

Championships when somebody leapt out and clubbed Kerrigan in the leg, attempting to put her out of action completely. Harding was under investigation, but was allowed to compete in the Olympics where she came nowhere and a recovered Kerrigan earned silver. Later, though, she admitted she'd been involved and was banned from amateur skating.

Eddie Edwards

Eddie Edwards of Great Britain was a one-man polar problem. In 1988, funding himself and without any formal training, he turned up for the Olympic ski-jump competition. His equipment was so dodgy that other skiers had a whip-round to get him some proper skis. He competed in both 70 m and 90 m events – and came a long way last in both. But did he become famous!

Here are just a few of the things said about Eddie. Fill in the blanks using these words:

clowns, crazy, eagle, fly, loser, sportsman

290. Rob McCormack, official in charge of the ski-jump competition: "Eddie doesn't .... He just drops out of the sky. It's not ski-jumping."

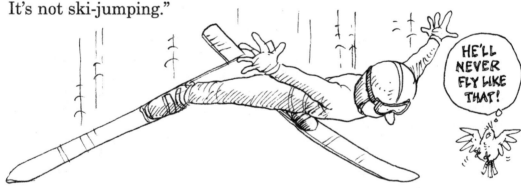

291. Finnish ski-jump star and gold medallist, Matti Nykänen: "You must not laugh at Eddie. He is good for our sport. We need some ...."

292. Julian Brand, a sports agent, explaining why Eddie became famous: "His appeal is because he is such a spectacular ...."

293. Everybody had their say about him, even darts player Eric Bristow: "Don't tell me he's a ....!"

294. At the closing ceremony, Eddie's nickname even got a mention in the President's closing speech: "At this Olympic Games some competitors have won gold and some have broken records, and one has even flown like an ...."

295. And what did Eddie himself say? "Everybody thinks I'm .... They're probably right."

Answers:

290. Fly.

291. Clowns.

292. Loser.

293. Sportsman. Bristow was trying to respond to criticism that darts wasn't a real sport.

294. Eagle.

295. Crazy.

But Eddie the Eagle had the last laugh. He became so well known that he made a small fortune from newspapers and TV when the Games were over. And he's still a star. When visitors to the Calgary site watch the commemorative video of the 1988 Winter Olympics, the longest slot they see is devoted to Eddie Edwards!

CLOSING CEREMONY

The Games are over. Soon it will be time to count your medals. But first, a final five questions. Will they help you on to the winner's podium?

Congratulations!
296. At the first modern Olympics in 1896, what did event winners receive?
a) A gold medal.
b) A silver medal.
c) A crown of olive leaves.

297. What did those finishing second receive in 1896?
a) A silver medal.
b) A bronze medal.
c) A crown of laurel leaves.

298. What did third-placed competitors receive in 1896?
a) A bronze medal.
b) Nothing.
c) A crown of oak leaves.

299. When did the competitors receive their medals?
a) After their event.
b) At the end of the Games.
c) After the Games.

300. Medal winners or not, all Olympic competitors are invited along to the Closing Ceremony. They hear speeches, see demonstrations, watch the Olympic flame being extinguished ... and sing a national anthem. But the anthem of which country?
a) Greece.
b) The country hosting the Games.
c) The country due to host the Games in four years' time.

Medal table

So, how did you do? Did you sprint to the finish or treat it as a marathon? Did you shoot a high score or dive to a low one?

You've faced 300 questions altogether. So step up and receive your award!

If your score was pretty rubbish then all I can say is that it's a good time to remember the words that were first displayed at the 1932 Olympics and have been given pride of place ever since. Baron de Coubertin had heard them at a church service and liked them.

"The most important thing is not to win but to take part, just as the most important thing in life is not the triumph but the struggle. The essential thing is not to have conquered but to have fought well."

They're what the Olympics should be all about – no question!